EARTH IN ANGER

EARTH IN ANGER

Twenty-Five Poems of Love and Despair

for Planet Earth

James P. Lenfestey

Red Dragonfly Press – Minnesota – 2013

ISBN 978-1-937693-25-1

ISBN 978-1-937693-26-8 (e-book)

Printed in the United States of America
on 30% recycled stock
by BookMobile, a 100% wind-powered company

Cover image: skeletonized maple leaf (photograph by Scott King)

Designed and Typeset by Scott King using Quadraat OT

Published by Red Dragonfly Press
press-in-residence at the Anderson Center
P. O. Box 406
Red Wing, MN 55066
www.reddragonflypress.org

CONTENTS

To
John Felstiner, author of
Can Poetry Save the Earth?
A Field Guide to Nature Poems
and
Bill McKibben
and 350.org

...Earth in anger
began each night to issue phantoms,
dreams to haunt mortals' sleep,
revealing how things really stand,
and what events are destined.

—Chorus, *Iphigenia in Tauris*, Euripides
translated by H. L. Hix

PREFACE

What would the world be, once bereft
Of wet and of wildness?
– Gerard Manley Hopkins, from 'Inversnaid'

The risk here is rhetoric. As Yeats said, "Out of a quarrel with others we make rhetoric, of the quarrel with ourselves, poetry." The risk did not stop my pen from scratching its hot fury, from refining molten grief. The offerings here represent an eruption over the past three or four years. The collection may not be for you, only for me. The poems will not soothe you, nor do they soothe me. Thoreau said, "A true account of the actual is the rarest poetry." But what if the "actual"—climate change, plummeting biodiversity, melting Arctic—has taken on near-mythic dimension? A ravenous giant stepping from the west with footprints of drought and storm? Or "the Devil himself" striding up with the dawn, "horned head hot with laughter?" How do we meet such monsters? How to cool the fire? How to sweeten with honey when we weep only salt?

Small answers lie inside. Big answers are for another time, another medium. As a journalist reporting the facts of climate science since 1988, nearly a quarter century, I have witnessed a Goebbels-like propaganda machine funded by coal, oil and gas interests, plus anti-regulatory ideologues, depress public understanding into apathy over the findings and alarms of climate science, even raising anger at the scientists themselves. This is criminal, not poetic, stuff. One flails desperately.

What would Whitman do? That I did, here.
What would Thoreau do?

James P. Lenfestey
Minneapolis, Minnesota
Fall, 2012

As always, my deepest gratitude to the Anderson Center for the time to assemble this manuscript, to Scott King for designing it, for Thomas R. Smith for his accurate editorial eye and similarly smoldering heart.

INVOCATION

A thousand shafts of light strike the forest floor.
I know, I counted them once or twice
before.

Am I a fool to count
a thousand shafts of light,
or am I right?

Come count with me,
O foolish ones,
and hear the songs
that seared my sight.

I CARRY THE GRIEF OF THE WORLD

And this is the condemnation: that Light is come into the world, and men loved
darkness rather than light.... JOHN 3:19

I carry the grief of the world
in a joyful body. What should I do?

I step out the door at dawn, pleased
to find the sun once again cool and friendly.

At evening, I retire to my hut
desperate and murderous,
the earth retiring in flames.

At midnight, the moon mocks
monks who see in her brave shine
cool enlightenment, not hot despair.

Soon enough, dawn will arrive
as the Devil himself
striding over the rim of the earth
horned head hot with laughter.

What witless pact we mortals signed
to gain the slave toiling inside our dishwashers,
lighting our way at night, amusing us to sleep.

I already feel the heat, the shame,
and it is not yet noon.

A HELLISH HOT DAY IN THE ANTHROPOCENE
(JULY 31, 2011)

A pair of Great Blue Herons, like sea monsters in funeral cassocks, rise over the bluff, two ominous silent prayers. This will be a very bad day, when the sun strikes the sea like a gong. The cedars wave their rags against unforgiving sky, a humid grief in which only crows row with vigor, sensing everywhere the dead and dying. Sharp-shin, that magician, lives darkly in the trees behind, chortling at dawn and dusk the success of his swoops. So many tourist birds pass by, not suspecting his claws, his shriek of surprise and delight. The jays do not like him at all, howling nasal alarms.

Yea, though I sit on the lip of the bluff, a dulled, humbled observer, fingers dancing like spider legs on webs, I fear all excess. Even you, dear reader, in your narrow room exhaling doom with every well-meant breath. Tell me, how will you spend this hellish hot day and the days beyond? What distant life will you too inadvertently destroy?

ANTHROPOCENE: Geological societies are currently debating changing the name of earth's current epoch from Holocene to Anthropocene, as major natural systems have been demonstrably altered by human activity, including climate, biodiversity, land use, ocean chemistry, and the carbon, nitrogen, and water cycles.

SKIN OF DUST

Flying over the great knobby spine of the country,
rising up snow-capped and drifting,
I see her skin of dust.

And in the three or four hours
it takes to pass over, I can believe
in the curvature below, that it is
natural, growing and sloughing
as it always has, like the old reptiles.

And that I do not need to grieve,
this heartbreak, as the grids
reveal themselves, the weeds of roads,
the pit mine's azure eye,
a vacant staring iris of water,
the cigarettes of cancerous smoking coal plants
("plant," as if erupting grass, a jonquil!)

The awful despoliation
around the great salt shadow of Utah
and Nevada's dead white bicarbonate lakes.

From up here, dinosaur earth greens,
skin ignoring her lesions, cancerous, terminal,
her rumbling gut, her gasps for wholesome breath.

A simple cloud floats below
leaving a lake of shade,
irregular as a carcinoma.

A PRAYER TO EL NIÑO ON BEHALF OF THE GEESE

Who hears the regrets of the thieving automobile?
– Pablo Neruda, *The Book of Questions, III*

El Niño, I pray to you on my
cracked and bleeding knees and
fully acknowledging my beloved grandfather
who brought the first car and airplane
(which would not fly)
to our small Wisconsin town,
and my father who sent ton after ton of
anthracite rattling down basement chutes
all over the county
so that I might have heat and books
and fly over the world, I pray
on behalf of today's confused geese
flying north in January, and mother bears
sniffing bleary-eyed at sprouting buds,
that El Niño's unaccountable winter torrents
wash clean the powerful men and women
fouling the only nest we will ever
know in this God's universe.

EAGLE AT 8AM

He leadeth me beside the still waters... Psalm 23.

Wings like dark scoops
press gustless dawn
to seize the bluff-bound branch,
his favorite perch, to strike
his cape of wings and raise the white flag
of his crown,
to stand between the plummet and the
time when even lazy predators

like you, like me, can be ourselves,
our regal myths a moment stayed
of stature, courage, free of greed,
before our plunge toward earth
to snatch whatever drifting gulls upturn
in ugly squabbles at the shore.

Ah eagle, we are brothers after all.
Not Franklin's higher view of us
as gobblers, eating only what the earth
provides, seed enough to keep
us clean and cared for.
No, we loiter on the bluff
in mighty profile, eyes right,
and

(cover your ears
with your shawl of wings)
steal everything.

Everything except what is, with God,
ungraspable. What is found
in psalms and poems and taut old strings—
taloned cellos, soaring violins.

SO MANY STARLINGS

I suppose I could say the flock
of a thousand starlings suddenly descended
like a storm lights up the day
with its electric clatter in the leaves,
like a million shattered plates, like sparks
from writhing, downed electric lines.

I suppose I could color them all
within the horizon lines belonging here—
the way you, my brothers and sisters, belong,
our cloud descended too like ruin
three centuries and more ago, but
who is counting?

So, my starlings, my loves, love me too
for who I am, your sluggish cousin
too close to marry but not desire.

So my starship, my darlings,
our dark shadows impervious to wind
descend like a celestial hammer,
rise like a kitchen disaster,
fly like a hail of bullets fired at Pickett's
Charge, at Normandy, or somewhere
in Afghanistan at some silly girl
who looked sideways at a man.

FALL OF A CORPSE OF A BIRD

I hoped it was a starling, those electronic annoyances,
or even a robin, magnificent thrush but familiar,
like a toothbrush. The cardinal has not sung today—
is it your whistle he ate?
Or the jay who screams all day,
astringent harridan? Was the thudding mass
dropped under the ostrich ferns wearing shiny
blue feathers, a breast of orange,
a cockscomb of red?

Sharp-shin, my love, shitting white streaks on my roof
like milkshakes, like dear swift magician Merlin,
I have caught you with only three sidelong glances—
a swooping course along the lawn
and two returns, white innocent underwings
hurtling hidden claws toward the spruce.
There you chitter and hide, chitter and hide,
dropping your victims' skins like gum wrappers,
thudding around me like mortars.

How happy I am it is you
cleansing the skies, and not me
with my exhaust of poisons, my food
delivered in wheezing trucks
from fields freed of birds in favor
of my own gargantuan appetite,
ruthless and irredeemable weed.

SPIDER TAKES DRAGONFLY, WASP TAKES SPIDER

In the abattoir off the front porch,
of lazy spirea and erotic flowers,
the ancient game plays out: dragonfly
takes gnat, spider takes dragonfly,
wasp takes spider.

In the corner above the faded flag
the hooked legs of spider entwine
the big-eyed darner too eager for his gnats,
while the darth vader wasp
drags his saber appendages
over the spider's defenseless lair.

In this old game of predator-prey,
who takes rock, takes scissors, takes wasp?
Only hungry humans know.
We will eat anything, break anything.
No creature, no planet safe from our
devouring, foolish hunters too busy playing
childhood games at the garden's edge
to glance toward the hot and hellish horizon.

SQUASHING A SPIDER

That life in my hand, where did it go?
The motor that drove eight crooked
legs under eight roving eyes, did it
enter my fingertips, that shiver
like touching a peach?

What a crude mistake you made,
sliding down the glacier of the tub,
trapped liked some Sherpa
without water, food gone,
the color of dirt, not snow.

And God above, shining down
in a red hat, white cloth in hand,
falling as fast as the lightning bolt
that missed him in last week's storm,
the one that devoured rocks,
that split the white pine into swords
of anger and despair.

And now, because the lightning
shattered the world but missed God,
he decided, deliberately and without
rancor, that it would be best
for you to die, and not starve,
for your pinprick of a heart
and your boneless body

to crush like a blueberry,
no defenses at all against
a living God policing
his household
like a rat.

ONCE WE WERE PREY

Spooked like horses, glass-eyed
at some sharp sound,
bolting toward the heedless cliff.

Once we slept in trees
where snakes uncoiled toward us
down a higher branch.

Now we are predators,
and nothing living we find
can frighten us, but

carpenter ants, termites,
angry bees, and the sun
rising every morning
in a rage.

THEN WE WERE THE PROVINCES

They the dukes and lords
buying our furs, wearing
them thick with flair around Paris,
London, Antwerp.

Princesses swathed in otter,
mink collars, dangling ermine tails,
Dukes wearing our skins for hats.

And all the while we were stealing
their brains—
their lordliness, their style,
subsisting on bodies left behind
piled rank along streambeds,
eating bite after ugly bite the roasted
swamp of skinned bodies,
sucking the marrow from
crushed skulls and shattered leg bones.

Against prevailing winds we sucked
out all their lives, so short an era, cost
barely two dozen billion tiny bodies,
fed the stink to our forests felled
in a last drunken slaughter.
Then fire.

Suddenly heiress Maria stumbled, high
heel hooked in the cracked parquet,

Watt invented the steam engine,
Horace Mann invented high school,
and we declared victory.

Now Universities built from shorn land
suck the brains of the entire planet
into the iCloud, and we are all suddenly
unhappy,
knowing too much.

WAILING WALL

Where is the Western Wall
for all of us to wail?

To crack our cheeks
and break our bones
against hot, Satanic winds?

Where are our dolmens,
our circle of upright stones,
our dark, diminished cave?

Our Pentagon, our Chinese
armies sweeping down from the north
or up from the dust?

The enemy surrounds us
even as we dream, remembering Eden,
Wisconsin before the drought.

Another day, another coal mine dug,
underground days measured out in rice grains.
Our heads beat against the seams while jackhammers
plunder every inch of atmosphere
until we, like choked Venusians, telescope our
longing outward toward distant orbs,
bluegreen and beautiful,
or back down the tunnel of time
to the ignorant Dark Ages
we call now.

APROPOS OF NOTHING

No thing. As in
zed or zero or hole.
Sundays without mass,
or anything without mass.

As a bird rattling its cage
for no reason, or a squirrel
chattering at nothing,
or a dog picking up his ears
as in a dream.

Or a ship
gliding through the Arctic
where there used to be ice
once, where there used to be
something.

THINKING OF JAMES WRIGHT

I was noticing the cedar
waxwings roosted like wicks
in the candelabra of the dead birch
and thinking of the poet James Wright.
Who never sat upright, but taught and drank
slumped like a wounded bear—
sad and raging against the lead
caught in his gut,
who took the shot for all us, innocents
and felons and poets and brown-eyed suicides.
Like the manic dragon of those animated movies
spearstruck and rearing under mighty wings and breath
of flame and smoke and a bellyful
of beauty and grievance until the thrashing
slows, and death, sweet as an Italian spring,
appears beneath his fallen wing,
some idiot David stupidly triumphant, waving.
Or as if Robert Frost appeared in old age,
wet hand grooming the pasture spring
clearing leaf after leaf after leaf,
rhyme and line repelling
grief after grief after grief.

"SLEEPERS, AWAKE"
– for Piper, who died young

The bald guitarist hunches over his belly
to pluck his guts. Heavy glasses fall from sweaty pate
to sweaty nose as taut strings let go.
The audience, ten of us, stuck to our pews by the heat
and some inchoate pull not to scream,
bathe in the baptismal of Bach,
black notes with white wings.
We applaud lightly
with the wings of our hands, thank you,
thank you, as we slide unconscious
toward forgiving ourselves
through the pain in our knees
and our failing sight.

CHURCH

We will arise and go now,
we who do these things,
marking every seven days
the way the moon does,
with a change of light.

The feeling is choral, as of wind
over grass hills of pews, songs
familiar as rain, worn
syllables washed by organ pipes,
by children in robes and babies
in long dresses, families stirred
as we weep at the dare
they have taken.

Here in the Sanctuary
we lean against supporting pews
basking like seals
hauled up out of roiling waters,
sun on our backs, pups snuggling
and bawling in the Sunday school,
sips of coffee and tea and juice
enough for all.

And when outside again, and soon enough,
the birds have not missed us, nor the bears.
Nor our friends in private song,
nor the stained glass waters sparkling.

ELEGY FOR THE STURGEON MOON
August, Lake Huron

There is no loneliness like theirs. — James Wright

How can you exist, your great pale scales
prehistoric, as if life, or something else, existed before.
You who live hundreds of years as if it were natural,
who wait to mate into your twenties,
swimming up these short thin rivers like sweetwater seals.

How they loved you before the pale ones came,
waiting with spears and nets and clubs each spring
to smoke and dry and eat your tired, erotic bodies.
How my ancestors threw you away.

This image is the worst:
Eight-foot bodies stacked like cord wood on beaches
or burned in stinking steamships
slinking out of the bays.

So old, at the bottom, so far away now,
quiet and out of sight, lonely
for your kind, and kindness,
not one in a hundred surviving from your holocaust.
There is no loneliness like yours.

The surface of your waters is placid today,
then raked by wind into bony scales. Somewhere
below, a few of you, indifferent, huge and armor plated,

but soft inside, piled with dunes of eggs big as blueberries,
clean up as much of the mess as you can find,
asking only of your hundred million years
a hundred million more.

Like the moon, who rises full tonight in your name,
your humped back rises from the lake
carrying your story out of the deep
and spilling it silver at our feet.
See her sad and shining face,
ancient, primitive, cold, almost out of reach.
There is no loneliness like ours.

I long to take you in my arms,
sea monster of my childhood,
at the cradle of your hatchery,
long to eat again your smoked, delicious sides.

Yesterday I swam the shallows of Sturgeon Bay,
a quiet sand arc sheltered by dunes and resurgent pines
named in memory of your abundance,
where you once gathered in a hundred
villages every spring to trade and sport.

I glide alone now in clear water—a few minnows,
two human children shrieking on the shore,
a human mother reading her human book.
And the primitive motion of the waves—
that, at least, eternal.

INDIAN SUMMER ON MACKINAC
October, Lake Huron

The sun wants to claim me,
rising lazy out of the lake like a banker,
bright and late, nearly eight.

As if the hydrangeas cared,
robed in purple against just this,
your late rising, early to bed.

Where are the Indians now?
Duck's in his hut carving canes.
Mrs. Green's sitting on a bench.

Oh sun, you have seen this coming,
dripping cash over us, gold and silver,
currency never gathered, never spent.

Why me a witness to your legal claim,
an old man dithering on an old porch,
refusing to move, waiting for snow.
In your presence we turn our face away,
one-eyed, tears streaming.

Oh sun, you have watched us so long,
Great Lakes rising and falling with your breath,
one hat white with ice, another the blue Silurian sea.

At nine, the neighbor's angry engine roars
ruin, ruin.
You tell us your own engine
one day will flicker out,
Earth and all her gods finally
humble and silent and spent.

DENSITY

Maniboajo Bay

Gulls cry, children shriek, ferries thrum
over the wave break,
a rhythmic tearing of silken cloth.

The density of the surge
rocks pebbles and thighs
in the heavy folds of the sea.

From the distant shore,
talons of cloud
claw the horizon
dragging dark feathers
of storm toward the beach.

Soon enough, soon enough,
the surf says, so swim now.
Swim away with the fish,
who do not hear such airy things.
For whom the density of water
limits the reach of ruin.

I SWAM A LONG TIME IN THE LAKE

I swam a long time in the Lake
alone, swam a sea of silent storms,

then crawled upon the slippery stones,
something deep inside me gone.

That old familiarity of womb,
effortless twist of liquid song,

forgetting, almost, the need to breathe,
eyes on undulant rocks below,

waves above like silken sheets,
and all around, empyrean—

surround of touch, a timeless now,
fathomless home, fathomless Heaven

where swords of sunlight disappear,
your gaze amazed at flowing hair,

your waving arms, your fishlike feet
reluctant ever to crawl again

the torrid, crumbling, landlocked streets.

PEWTER MORNING

All is still upon the lake.
So still the sun melts moonlit night
to pewter nearly hard as steel
yet soft as silken sheets.

A freighter passes by, slices
the surface with its scissors prow,
off toward Duluth for grain
enough to feed a city for a year.

The surface in its wisdom heals.
And you and I, still here
upon our ragged bluff,
dine with the pewter surface
of the sun, the silver
memory of the moon.

And for a moment's gaze,
feel full enough.

HEAVEN
– for Jodey

Have you heard August's
surf on Superior's south shore
pounding pebbles like a glass hammer,
striking sonic booms three seconds apart.

We roll in the wave break,
clutching our knees in the swells,
listening... to the click,
grate, rattle and scrub of time,
sand grains built tick by tick
from blocks of black basalt,
granite veins, sandstone, chert,

rock remains tumbled, polished here
since glacial ice ground up and back
this canted swale where

my wife, my partner, lies in the palm
of beach and dune, in scoop and sweep
of grains at angle of repose.

I love the snow, its irregular
impossibility of flakes said ever
to differ even in banks
where we make angels.

But sand, warm under flanks
on twelve-mile beach
empty but for stragglers, seekers,
castaway feathers and airy bones...

This is what bodies dream of.
This is where bodies fall in love.

BUTTERFLY SONG

"Some people think butterflies sing to them, but I haven't heard it."
– Robert Michael Pyle

Near the garden in August, so loud
the singing. The near screams of the roses
and the tiny basso of the snapdragons,
you must settle under them to listen,
the bassoons of the cardinal flowers,
flutes of so many honeysuckle,
guitars of vines, and everywhere
clanging cymbals of leaf and petal.

Then the run of applause from the skies
pouring down like honey on frantic wings,
the drum corps of bees, many different sizes, the solo
snare of the bumbler, big as a thumb and as funny,
the giant hummer rolling and fading his pointed beats
behind his electric neck and long sharp tongue,
the beetles with spots and loud carapaces lifting off,
all of them strumming the taut tympanum of
humid summer air.

Then out of the high skies, down and down
on spastic wings that scream *impossible*,
sculpted square-rigged sails, phantom cloaks,
stunning spinnakers, lazy lifters, veins and scales,
silence without stillness, to listen

is to note the root tremble of all song,
without voice, without flute or grumble,
without sigh or anger or clang, but pure fluttering hunger
fallen from the symphony of cloud and sky
to settle delicate on the extended fingertip of the ear.

TWENTY DRUNKEN ROBINS
—for Robert Hedin

This I have never seen before:
a flock of twenty drunken robins
like happy children roiling the dusty
quilt of fallen oak leaves in October,
happy and chasing and free
under a red berry tree.

They are fat, and many, and young ones.
And I must say happy again,
loud songs waking late sleepers,
their leaf dance rustling up a racket,
so many bright berries this year of drought.

As if two leaves suddenly flown up,
two fledglings drunkenly cavort
in the nearby yew, then pause
like eager children in a game of tag,
white spectacles framing ecstatic gleams.

Then flutter back to the bar of berries,
raising as they alight in leaves their charcoal cloaks
trimmed ermine white
to dazzle me.

What a happy scene, this berry tree
I did not know, but robins do, rising

from tanned leather bur oak leaves
fallen here like prints of paws of bears
thick as a feather mattress where
happy inebriate native birds dive in flurries.

My friend tended this berry tree
a decade and a half
for these fresh thrush friends
to find and drink today,
and drunken, gladden me.

BY AZURE HURON'S SHORE

An update of Walt Whitman's "By Blue Ontario's Shore," section 12

AUTHOR'S NOTE: In 1848 journalist Walt Whitman and his fourteen year-old brother Jeff traveled to New Orleans to help establish the newspaper the *Crescent*. After three months, according to his own hand-drawn map now in the Library of Congress, they returned up the Mississippi and through the Great Lakes, passing through the Straits of Mackinac into Lake Huron, then Erie, then Ontario. In the 1867 edition of "Leaves of Grass" he included "As I Sat Alone By Blue Ontario's Shores," in which he encounters a "Phantom" who quizzes him on the qualities necessary to undertake the American project of creating and healing a nation. Inspired by Whitman's interrogation, I wondered what "many and stern" questions the Phantom would put to poets and citizens today to undertake our necessary project, healing and reclaiming our broken, reeling planet. In the Invocation, I changed but one word of Whitman's, substituting "earth" for "nation." The rest of the Phantom's interrogation came fresh through me in one burst as I sat alone by azure Huron's shore. Initially published as a broadside, "By Azure Huron's Shore" may be reproduced free forever.

INVOCATION

Are you he who would assume a place to teach or be a poet here on this earth?
The place is august, the terms obdurate.
Who would assume to teach here may well prepare himself body and mind,
He may well survey, ponder, arm, fortify, harden, make lithe himself.
He shall surely be questioned beforehand by me with many and stern questions.
Who are you indeed who would talk and sing of the earth?

⋆ ⋆ ⋆

Do you know the depth of the waters, and the height of the sky, and their composition?
Have you befriended the trees where you live, know their roots, their crowns?
Have you studied the rocks beneath them, to the fifth epoch?
And the birds above, their songs and what they eat, and where they nest?
And the people who lived there before you, and your ancestors, to the second
millennium?
And the rivers and lakes, their subtle watersheds and hidden springs?
And do you swim in the chill and warm waters of your seas and lakes indiscriminately?
And with relish? And know the sources of pollutants threatening your waters? And
fight against the dark rain with armies of petitions and voters' guides and drives and
meetings?

Are the glaciers and the jungles your friends, the serpents and beasts and birds your
guides, the pigs of the sty your helpmates, the microbes and fungi your intimates?
Do you shun or reform all religions that deny the primacy of the earth and its
processes? That believe mankind unable to destroy everything good? Or save everything
good?
Do you accept with joy the findings of science?

41

Are your taxes paid to the federal, state and municipal authorities without complaint, as the recognized price of civil living? Do you wish to pay more?

Do you believe in the Holy Trinity: The Water, The Grass, The Air? And do you worship them every day with acts of kindness and political clout?
Are you sickened unto death that the biodiversity of the earth is plummeting? The Arctic sea ice melting? The oceans acidifying?
Have you read the 4th Assessment of the Intergovernmental Panel on Climate Change? Or at least the Executive Summary?
And know that its finding of warming for the most part due to the burning of fossil fuels has been everywhere affirmed, including by the National Academy of Sciences, the National Research Council, even the George W. Bush Administration?
And are you hot with anger at the lies about the cause of changing climate spouted by those with fingers black with oil, breath black from smoking mines?
And will you slay with dark thoughts the miscreants at Fox News and the Wall Street Journal editorial page and Rush Windbag and others who perpetuate those lies?
Will you fight back with evidence and heat and love for the atmosphere which is the life blanket of our planet?

Do you firmly believe there is no such thing as evil, but only abundant ignorance, stupidity, shortsightedness, self-dealing, self-loathing and fundamentalist self-righteousness?
Do you "fear a lie as others fear fire," as Chekhov said, and know that "inside you is an inexhaustible fountain of ideas," as Brenda Ueland said?
Do you believe in families and communities green and cheerful with good schools and happy parents and joy shouted from the schoolyards?
Have your studied Emerson's essays The Poet and Nature, foundation stones of the spiritual democracy of our nation and all nations, who saw the divine in every person and particular of nature, including these Great Lakes? He who begat Thoreau and

Whitman and Dickinson and Bogan?
When you gaze at the person you love, and the multitudes you love, do tears of
gratitude spring to your eyes? Do your hands fall open in gratitude to the waters, the
grass, the air? And for people who fight for the waters, the grass, the air?

By azure Huron's shore,
do you stand at the water's edge, tasting the delicious energies of the grass, inhaling
the delicious energies of the air, and fearlessly plunge into the dark waters, for the sake
of your soul, and the soul of the earth?

CODA: TEACH THE CHILDREN

Our first home is water.
How grateful they are,
picnics at the beach,
sand in sandwiches,
toes at the water's edge.
Then knees, waist, heart, hair,
eyes open in wavering light.

ABOUT THE AUTHOR

James P. Lenfestey is a former editorial writer for the *StarTribune*, where he won several Page One Awards for excellence. Since 2000, he has published a collection of personal essays, a poetry anthology, four collections of his own poems, and co-edited *Robert Bly in This World*, University of Minnesota Press. As a journalist he had covered energy policy since 1975 and climate science since 1988. He lives in Minneapolis with his wife of 46 years, the political activist Susan Lenfestey. They have four children and six grandchildren.